BY ELSPETH CAMPBELL MURPHY
ILLUSTRATED BY JANE E. NELSON

SOMETIMES I GET SCARED

Printed in the United States of America.
ISBN: 0-89191-275-4
LC: 80-66534

SCARED

Do you know what you remind me of, God? A shepherd. You are strong and kind, and I am your little sheep. A shepherd takes good care of his sheep, and you take good care of me.

A shepherd helps his sheep find sweet, green grass to eat and cool, quiet water to drink. I don't eat grass. And I don't drink from quiet pools the way sheep do.

But I know how the sheep feel when their shepherd is nearby watching over them. They feel safe and happy. And I feel safe and happy when I remember that you are nearby watching over me.

The sheep don't know where to go or what to do, so their shepherd has to lead them and tell them to be good.

I don't always know what I should do, either. But I know you want me to be good. And I know you will help me, the way the shepherd helps his sheep.

VER SHOP
OPEN
9:00-5:00
PLANTS
SALE
FRESH
PRODUCE
NO
PARKING

Sometimes the sheep eat up all the grass in one good place, and the shepherd knows they have to move on.

And sometimes, to get there, the sheep have to go through a scary place—maybe a deep, narrow canyon with high, rocky walls.

And the sheep don't like it.

Well, I know how those sheep feel, because sometimes I get scared, too.

I don't like it when dogs bark at me. Or when the thunder is really loud. Or when I fall down and hurt myself. Or when I dream about monsters. Or when I think no one will play with me.

But when the sheep get scared, you know what? The shepherd taps them gently with his cane and says, "Don't be scared, sheep. It's all right. I'm here."

And that's the way you are, too, God. When I'm scared, it's like you are saying, "Don't be scared, little lamb. It's all right. I'm here."

You are so nice to me, God. You make me feel like it's always my birthday, and you are giving me a BIG party.

You are so good, and you love me so much.
Someday I will go to heaven to live with you.
And we will be together and love each other forever,
and ever,
and ever,
and EVER!